Key Stage 2

Reading and Writing Poetry

Carol Matchett

Name _____

Schofield & Sims

Introduction

Poetry is fun. Rhyme, rhythm, sound effects and language patterns make it different from any other form of writing. When you *write* poems, you put your ideas, feelings and experiences into words. When you *read* poems, you see the world through someone else's eyes.

This book starts by looking at different features of poetry, giving examples that show how they can make a poem effective. The book then looks at poetic forms. There are plenty of ideas for writing your own poems – and lots of tips that will help you to make your poems sound great!

Finding your way around this book

Before you start using this book, write your name in the name box on the first page. Then decide how to begin. If you want a complete course on reading and writing poetry, you should work right through the book from beginning to end.

Another way to use the book is to dip into it when you want to find out about a particular topic. The contents page will help you to find the pages you need. Whichever way you choose, don't try to do too much at once – it's better to work through the book in short bursts.

When you have found the topic you want to study, look out for these icons, which mark different parts of the text.

Activities

This icon shows you the activities that you should complete – you write in the spaces provided. This book does not include answers to the activities because there are so many different possible answers and it wouldn't be practical to list all of them. Check your answers with an adult and when you are sure that you understand the topic, put a tick in the box beside it on the Contents page. On page 32 you will find suggestions for some projects (**Now you try!**), which will give you even more opportunities to improve your understanding of poetry.

Explanation

This text explains the topic and gives examples. Read it before you start the activities.

Notes

Some extra things that you need to know.

Information

This text gives you background information about the history of poetry. Surprise your friends with some fascinating facts!

Contents

Tick the box when you have worked through the topic.

Rhyme

Rhyme is when words **end** with the **same sound. For example:**

hill   fill   will   kill   Jill   Bill   still

Poets often use rhyme to make **sound patterns** in their poems, but a poem does not *have* to rhyme. Often you will find the rhyming words at the **end of lines**, but sometimes words that rhyme are found **within a line** of the poem.

I. As you read these poems, listen for words that **rhyme**. Which poem does **not rhyme**?

In each **rhyming** poem, use different colours to circle words that rhyme.

On my Way to School

Thumping, bumping, jumping
Nipping, tripping, skipping
On my way to school.

Clopping, stopping, hopping
Stalking, talking, walking
On my way to school.

Anon

From The Echoing Green

The sun does arise,
And make happy the skies;
The merry bells ring
To welcome the Spring;
The skylark and thrush,
The birds of the bush,
Sing louder around
To the bells' cheerful sound;
While our sports shall be seen
On the echoing green.

By **William Blake** *(1757–1827)*

Windy Nights

Whenever the moon and stars are set,
    Whenever the wind is high,
All night long in the dark and wet,
    A man goes riding by.
Late in the night when the fires are out,
Why does he gallop and gallop about?

Whenever the trees are crying aloud,
    And the ships are tossed at sea,
By, on the highway, low and loud,
    By at the gallop goes he.
By at the gallop he goes and then
By he comes back at the gallop again.

By **Robert Louis Stevenson** *(1850–1894)*

Roses are red
Violets are blue
Some poems rhyme
This one doesn't.

Anon

Rhyme patterns

There are many different **rhyme patterns**. Sometimes two lines that follow each other will end with rhyming words. **For example:**

The Sun does **arise**
And make happy the **skies**

◀ This is called a **rhyming couplet** because a **couple** of lines rhyme.

Sometimes there is another line between the lines that rhyme. **For example:**

On goes the river
And out past the **mill**,
Away down the valley,
Away down the **hill**.

1. Read these poems and think about the **rhyme pattern**. Then read the labels in the boxes on the right, and match the correct label to each poem.

In a Jam

Sitting here waiting in a traffic jam
Makes me think how impatient I am.

Anon

This poem is written in rhyming couplets.

From Where go the Boats?

Dark brown is the river,
Golden is the sand.
It flows along for ever,
With trees on either hand.

By **Robert Louis Stevenson** (1850–1894)

This poem is just one rhyming couplet.

From In the Summer

In the summer when I go to bed
The sun still streaming overhead
My bed becomes so small and hot
With sheets and pillow in a knot
And then I lie and try to see
The things I'd really like to be.

By **Thomas Hood** (1799–1845)

In this poem, there is another line between the rhyming lines.

2. Look at the poem 'Windy Nights' on page 4. What do you notice about the **rhyme pattern**?

_____

_____

Rhyming couplets

Rhyme is sometimes obvious and sometimes hidden. When you are reading a poem aloud, it is important to pay attention to the rhyming pattern. Does the poet want you to stress the rhyme, or play it down?

With poems written in **rhyming couplets**, we tend to pause slightly at the end of each **line** to **stress the rhyme**.

1. This poem is written in **rhyming couplets** but the writer has forgotten to put in the line breaks. Read the words aloud. Listen for the **rhyme** that shows where the line breaks should be.

When I first awake all I hear are birds singing both far and near.
But then the house fills up with noise – TVs, shouts and electronic toys.

Write the poem with the line breaks. It should be four lines long.

_____

_____

_____

_____

2. Here is the first verse from a poem called 'The Moon', which is written in **rhyming couplets. But only the first line is in the right place** – all the other lines are in the wrong order! Write the verse with the lines in the right order. Read it aloud to check it makes sense.

The moon has a face like the clock in the hall;
On streets and fields and harbour quays,
And birdies asleep in the forks of the trees.
She shines on thieves on the garden wall,

***Muddled-up extract from* The Moon**

By **Robert Louis Stevenson** (1850–1894)

The moon has a face like the clock in the hall;

_____

_____

_____

Writing a number rhyme

Writing rhyming poems can be difficult. You have to find words that rhyme *and* make sure that your poem makes sense. You might need to think of lots of ideas before you find a version that sounds right, so try out your ideas in rough first.

It is a good idea to start off by writing a poem that follows a simple **pattern**.

1. Here is the start of a **number rhyme**. Finish the poem by writing the rest of the **rhyming couplets**. Keep reading your poem aloud to make sure it sounds right and makes sense.

Ten dogs in the park
One of them began to bark.

Five goats go to town
One of them _____

Nine monkeys in a tree
One of them laughed at me.

Four _____ by the door
One of them _____

Eight cows on a hill
One of them _____

Three_____
One of them _____

Seven sheep in the street
One of them _____

Two_____
One of them _____

Six birds in the sky
One of them _____

One duck all alone
All the others _____

Did you know... Poetry was originally composed to be spoken, sung or chanted, rather than written down. This is why rhyme, rhythm and other sound patterns have always been so important in poetry. Some of the oldest forms of poetry, such as sonnets and ballads, had fixed rhyme patterns that all poets were expected to stick to. Today, poets tend to use rhyme much more freely – or not at all.

Rhythm

Rhythm is important in poems. **Rhythm** is the **beat** of the words that you can feel when you read a poem aloud. Some poems have a very strong rhythm with the same number of beats in each line of the poem. **For example:**

> Tyger! Tyger! Burning bright
> In the forests of the night

There are seven syllables in each of these lines, and they help to give the poem a strong rhythm.
The lines are taken from a poem by William Blake (1757–1827).

1. Here is an extract from a long poem called 'The Song of Hiawatha'. In this part of the poem, the spirit Gitche Manito is speaking to the people, warning them to stop fighting and to live in peace.

Read the poem aloud and feel the **rhythm** or **beat** of the words.

Then, count the number of syllables in the lines that are marked. What do you notice?

From The Song of Hiawatha

I have given you lands to hunt in,
I have given you streams to fish in,
I have given you bear and bison,
I have given you roe and reindeer,
I have given you brant and beaver,
Filled the marshes full of wild-fowl,
Filled the rivers full of fishes;
Why then are you not contented?
Why then will you hunt each other?

I am weary of your quarrels,
Weary of your wars and bloodshed,
Weary of your prayers for vengeance,
Of your wranglings and dissensions;
All your strength is in your union,
All your danger is in discord;
Therefore be at peace henceforward,
And as brothers live together.

By **Henry Wadsworth Longfellow** (1807–1882)

☐ syllables

☐ syllables

☐ syllables

☐ syllables

☐ syllables

2. Some words and phrases are used over and over again. This helps to make the **rhythm** even stronger. Underline words and phrases that are **repeated** in the poem.

Rhythm

Some forms of poetry should be **read aloud**, or **performed**, rather than read quietly. Rap poems, for example, have a particularly strong **rhythm**. As you listen to a rap poem, you will feel the rhythm and **beat** in each line. You can clap your hands, stamp your feet or click your fingers to the beat.

1. Here is a **rap** poem with a **strong rhythm**. Read the poem aloud and feel the **beat**. There are four strong beats in each line. Like this:

The **dis**co **sheep** danced **down** the **street**.

The Disco Sheep

The disco sheep danced down the street.
He stomped his hooves to a disco bleat.

'I'm Sam the Ram. So form a queue.
I'll dance with ewe and ewe and ewe.

'I'm the best at The Hip Hop Skip.
Your number one at The Sheep Dip Trip.

'All you sheep wherever you are,
Shout Sam the Ram – Superbaah.'

By **John Coldwell**

2. The poem makes you smile. Explain what makes these words and phrases funny.

a disco bleat _____

with ewe and ewe and ewe _____

Superbaah _____

All rap poetry is meant to be performed. This goes back to its origins in Jamaica and other Caribbean countries, where it drew on the rhythms and beat of the local music. Before that, the history of rap can be traced back to Africa, where poetry, music and dance were combined to perform stories about the history of an area.

Rhythm and rhyme

In many poems the **rhythm** and **rhyme** work together to give the overall 'sound' of the poem. When you are reading a poem aloud it is important to follow both the rhythm and the rhyme to make your reading of the poem effective.

1. Here is a poem with a strong rhythm and rhyme. Practise reading it aloud. Underline the **strong beats** in the poem as you read it.

From The Ghosts' High Noon

When the <u>night</u> wind <u>howls</u> in the <u>chimney</u> <u>cowls</u>, and
    the <u>bat</u> in the <u>moonlight</u> <u>flies</u>,
And inky clouds, like funeral shrouds, sail over the
    midnight skies –
When the footpads quail at the night-bird's wail, and
    the black dogs bay at the moon,
Then is the spectres' holiday – then is the ghosts' high noon!

As the sob of the breeze sweeps over the trees, and the
    mists lie low on the fen,
From grey tombstones are gathered the bones that once
    were women and men,
And away they go, with a mop and a mow, to the revel that
    ends too soon,
For cockcrow limits our holiday – the dead of the night's
    high noon!

By **W.S. Gilbert** (1836–1911)

2. Here is the first part of the poem again. Use different colours to circle the words that **rhyme**. Check if the rest of the poem follows the same **rhyme pattern**.

When the night wind (howls) in the chimney (cowls), and

the bat in the moonlight flies,

And inky clouds, like funeral shrouds, sail over the

midnight skies –

Writing a poem with rhythm

When you are writing a poem, you must keep reading it **aloud** to check the **rhythm**. When you read it aloud, you will immediately tell if you have lost the rhythm, as the poem will not sound right.

For example: Poems are cool, poems are fine,
Poems have rhythm and also there are lots of them that rhyme.

The last part of this is much too long – it doesn't flow.

Poems are cool, poems are fine;
Poems have rhythm, they also have rhyme.

This sounds much better.

1. Here is the start of a poem called 'The Animal Rap'. See if you can complete the poem keeping the strong **rhythm** and **rhyme**.

The Animal Rap

We can stamp, we can clap,

We can do the animal rap.

We can jump, we can hop,

We can do the kangaroo bop.

We can _____, we can _____

We can do the _____ fling.

> You need a word that rhymes with 'fling'.

We can _____, we can _____

We can do the _____ jive.

> You need the name of an animal. Don't choose a word with only one syllable as it will spoil the rhythm. A word with three syllables would be best.

We can _____, we can _____

We can do the _____ .

Sound effects – alliteration

As well as having rhyme and rhythm, poems may also have other **sound effects**. Poets will often put together words with **similar sounds** in order to make interesting effects. **Alliteration** is when you put together words **beginning with the same sound**.

For example: No **s**tir in the air, no **s**tir in the **s**ea;
The **s**hip was as **s**till as she could be;

Assonance is when you put together words with the **same vowel sound**.

For example: Betw**ee**n the tr**ee**s thr**ee** men were s**ee**n

I. Here are two poems that use interesting **sound effects**. Read the poems and listen for words that have the **same sound**. Underline these words.

The Eagle

He clasps the crag with crooked hands;
Close to the sun in lonely lands,
Ringed with the azure world, he stands.

The wrinkled sea beneath him crawls;
He watches from his mountain walls,
And like a thunderbolt he falls.

By **Alfred, Lord Tennyson** (1809–1892)

From The Jumblies

They went to sea in a Sieve, they did,
In a Sieve they went to sea;
In spite of all their friends could say,
On a winter's morn, on a stormy day,
In a Sieve they went to sea!
And when the Sieve turned round and round,
And everyone cried, 'You'll all be drowned!'
They called aloud, 'Our Sieve ain't big,
But we don't care a button! We don't care a fig!
  In a sieve we'll go to sea!'
    Far and few, far and few,
      Are the lands where the Jumblies live;
    Their heads are green, and their hands are blue,
      And they went to sea in a Sieve.

By **Edward Lear** (1812–1888)

Writing a poem using alliteration

Using alliteration is fun. The main problem tends to be that you find yourself using it too much! This can rather spoil the effect. To give yourself a feel for how alliteration can work, try writing an alliterative poem.

I. Here is the start of an alliterative poem. See if you can complete the other lines of the poem by choosing words beginning with the same sound.

It's a Mystery

One <u>d</u>ark and <u>d</u>reary <u>d</u>ay

To a <u>s</u>ilent, <u>s</u>leepy <u>s</u>treet

<u>C</u>ame a <u>c</u>lanking, <u>c</u>lattering <u>c</u>arriage.

From the <u>c</u>lanking, <u>c</u>lattering <u>c</u>arriage

Stepped a f_____ , f_____ figure

<u>C</u>arrying a _____ , _____ case

The _____ , _____ figure

Studied all the _____ and _____ <u>d</u>oorways

With a _____ , _____ <u>s</u>tare.

Then this _____ and _____ <u>s</u>omeone

Returned to the _____ , _____ <u>c</u>arriage

And <u>d</u>isappeared into the _____ and _____ <u>d</u>ay.

The use of alliteration in poems is even older than the use of rhyme.
Until the thirteenth century, alliteration and assonance were much more common in poems than rhyme.

Images – similes and metaphors

Descriptive poems often include images. An **image** makes a **picture** in the reader's mind by **comparing** the thing being described with something else. A **simile** is an image that uses the words *like* or *as*.

For example:

> The moon has a face **like** the clock in the hall;

Here the simile compares the shape of the moon's face with the face of a clock.

A **metaphor** does **not** use the words *like* or *as*. **For example:**

> the Sun **is** an orange dinghy

1. Here is an extract from a poem. Underline the **simile** used in the extract. In the box, explain why the poet chose that simile.

From O Wind

I saw you toss the kites on high
And blow the birds about the sky;
And all around I heard you pass,
Like ladies' skirts across the grass

By **Robert Louis Stevenson** (1850–1894)

> The simile describes

2. Here is a poem made up of a list of **metaphors**. Read the poem. In the thought bubble, write or draw what the poem makes you **picture**.

What... is the Sun?

the Sun is an orange dinghy
    sailing across a calm sea

it is a gold coin
    dropped down a drain in Heaven

the Sun is a yellow beach ball
    kicked high into the summer sky

it is a red thumb-print
    on a sheet of pale blue paper

the sun is a milk bottle's gold top
    floating in a puddle

By **Wes Magee**

Writing a poem using metaphors

You can change a simple **simile** into a more interesting **metaphor**. For example, in the poem 'What ... is the Sun?' (page 14) the poet takes the **simile**:

> the Sun is *like* an orange dinghy

and turns it into a longer **metaphor**

> the Sun is an orange dinghy
> sailing across a calm sea

Notice that in the **metaphor** the poet does not use the word *like* to make the comparison.

1. Write your own **metaphor list poem** based on the poem 'What ... is the Sun?'

Choose one of the following for the subject of your poem:

| rain | night | moon | Earth |

Start by thinking of five **similes** and then make each simile into a longer **metaphor**.

What is the _____ ?

the _____ is a _____

_____

it is _____

_____

the _____ is a _____

_____

it is a _____

_____

the _____ is a _____

_____

Poets often use **personification**. This simply means describing an object or an idea as if it were a person. **For example:**

Angry lightning cracked its whip across the sky

Here the poet describes lightning as if it were a person, with human actions and feelings.

1. Here is an extract from a poem that describes the season winter as if it were a person. Read the extract and in the box draw 'Winter', as described in this part of the poem.

From December

A wrinkled crabbed man they picture thee,
Old Winter, with a rugged beard as grey
As the long moss upon the apple-tree;
Blue-lipt, an ice drop at thy sharp blue nose,
Close muffled up, and on thy dreary way
Plodding along through sleet and drifting snows.

By **Robert Southey** *(1774–1843)*

2. In the next poem the poet describes different sorts of weather as if they are people. Circle the **adjectives** used to describe each type of weather. Then underline the words that describe how each type of weather **behaves**.

Weathers

Weathers are moody:
Hyperactive Wind
is never still;
Wet Fog
just hangs around;
Ebullient Hail
bounces back.

Rain doesn't muck about:
he's down to earth.

By **Michael Harrison**

ebullient – happy, cheerful.

Writing a poem using personification

You can use personification to help you describe things in poems. Think of subjects as if they were people and then decide what sort of people they would be, what they would look like and how they would behave.

1. In the poem 'December' (page 16), Robert Southey describes winter as a wrinkled old man. What sort of person do you think the other seasons would be?

Choose one of the other seasons and imagine it as a person. Tick the season you are thinking about and write your ideas in the boxes.

What sort of person is this season?
Old or young? Man or woman?

Behaviour
How does your chosen season behave? What does it do?

Spring ☐   **Summer** ☐   **Autumn** ☐

Appearance
What does this season look like? What clothes is it wearing?

Mood, feelings, qualities
Describe the character of this season.

2. Now use your ideas about your chosen season to write a poem – on a separate piece of paper.

You could start with the line:

Here comes _____ dressed in his/her _____

Responding to poems on a theme

Lots of poets write about the **same subject**, but they write about it in their own way and using their own **style**. Each poet's view of the subject will be different and so each poem will be unique. Some poets like to write poems with a strict pattern. Others prefer to be much freer with their words and with the shape of the poem.

1. On these two pages you will find three poems about the sea.

Read each of the poems and write your thoughts and ideas in the space provided.

On the Beach

The waves claw
At the shingle
Time after time.
They fall back
Again and again,
Sighing, sighing.

By **Michael Harrison**

> When I read this poem I picture

Until I Saw the Sea

Until I saw the sea
I did not know
that wind
could wrinkle water so.

I never knew
that sun
could splinter a whole sea of blue.

Nor
did I know before
a sea breathes in and out
upon a shore.

By **Lilian Moore**

> Here the poet is describing

> The poet is describing

> The poet is describing

Responding to poems on a theme

The Tide Rises, the Tide Falls

The tide rises, the tide falls,
The twilight darkens, the **curlew** calls;
Along the sea-sands damp and brown
The traveller hastens towards the town,
   And the tide rises, the tide falls.

Darkness settles on roofs and walls,
But the sea, the sea in the darkness calls;
The little waves, with their soft white hands,
Efface the footprints in the sands,
   And the tide rises, the tide falls.

The morning breaks; the **steeds** in their stalls
Stamp and neigh, as the **hostler** calls;
The day returns, but nevermore
Returns the traveller to the shore,
   And the tide rises, the tide falls.

By **Henry Wadsworth Longfellow** (1807–1882)

notes

curlew – a type of bird.
steeds – horses.
hostler – someone who works
at a stables.

This poem is about

2. Read the poems again. Underline the words and phrases that you find most effective.

3. Read the poems again and compare these features:

	On the Beach	Until I Saw the Sea	The Tide Rises, the Tide Falls
Use of rhyme			
Sound patterns			
The pattern or shape of the poem			

Writing about poems

When writing about a poem you need to say **what the poem is about** and **what makes it effective**. You should point out features of the poem, such as rhyme or other sound patterns, say whether it has a strong rhythm, and give examples of images or effective words and phrases.

1. Choose one of the poems about the sea to write about. Use the notes you made on the previous pages to help you complete this commentary on the poem.

Title of the poem:

What the poem is about:

Form and features of the poem (for example, rhyme, rhythm, sound patterns, repeated patterns):

Examples of effective words and phrases (and why they were chosen):

What I like or dislike about the poem and what makes it effective:

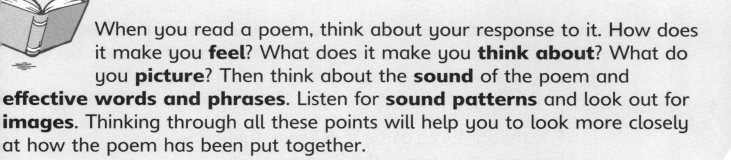

Thinking about a poem

When you read a poem, think about your response to it. How does it make you **feel**? What does it make you **think about**? What do you **picture**? Then think about the **sound** of the poem and **effective words and phrases**. Listen for **sound patterns** and look out for **images**. Thinking through all these points will help you to look more closely at how the poem has been put together.

I. Here is a poem for you to read and think about. Read the poem and write your **thoughts** and **ideas** in the thought bubbles. Don't worry if there is the odd word or line that you don't understand – just think about the general mood and the picture that you get from the poem.

No!

No sun – no moon!
No morn – no noon –
No dawn – no dusk – no proper time of day –
No sky – no earthly view –
No distance looking blue –
No road – no street – no 't'other side the way' –
No top to any steeple –
No recognitions of familiar people –
No courtesies for showing 'em –
No knowing 'em!
No travelling at all – no locomotion –
No inkling of the way – no notion –
'No go' – by land or ocean –
No mail – no post –
No news from any foreign coast –
No park – no ring – no afternoon gentility –
No company – no nobility –
No warmth, no cheerfulness, no healthful ease,
No comfortable feel in any member –
No shade, no shine, no butterflies, no bees,
No fruits, no flowers, no leaves, no birds.
November!

By **Thomas Hood** (1799–1845)

The poem makes me feel

The poem makes me picture

The poem makes me think about

What I like about this poem is

Nonsense poetry

A **nonsense poem** sounds funny and makes you smile. The words have been chosen because they sound amusing, rather than because they make sense.

For example:

> For the <u>Jumblies</u> came in a Sieve, they did,
> Landing at eve near the <u>Zemmery Fidd</u>
> Where the <u>Oblong Oysters</u> grow
>
> By **Edward Lear** (1812–1888)

Nonsense poems often contain words that don't exist – the poet has made them up just for the poem!

1. Here is a **nonsense poem** that mentions strange imaginary animals. Read the poem and underline the made-up **nonsense words**.

***From* A Quadrupedremian Song**

He dreamt that he saw the Buffalant,
    And the spottified Dromedaraffe,
The blue Camelotamus, lean and gaunt,
    And the wild Tigeroceros calf.

The maned Liodillo loudly roared,
    And the Peccarbok whistled its whine,
The Chinchayak leapt on the dewy sward,
    As it hunted the pale Baboopine.

By **Thomas Hood the Younger** (1835–1874)

2. Names of real animals have been put together to make the names of these imaginary animals. Complete the word sums to show how the animal names were made up.

Baboopine = | *baboon* | + | *porcupine* |

Buffalant = | | + | |

Camelotamus = | | + | |

Tigeroceros = | | + | |

Liodillo = | | + | |

Writing a nonsense poem

Writing a **nonsense poem** can be fun. You can make up lots of strange words. Nonsense poems usually have a very strong rhythm and rhyme, so keep reading your poem aloud to make sure that it sounds right.

1. Make up your own **nonsense poem** based on 'A Quadrupedremian Song' (opposite). First, make up eight strange animals by mixing up parts of the names of these real animals.

hippop	otamus

rhin	oceros

croc	odile

kang	aroo

ant	elope

flam	ingo

eleph	ant

chimp	anzee

wolf	lion

_____   _____   _____   _____

_____   _____   _____   _____

2. Now fit the names of the animals into this poem.

My Animal Dream

I dreamt that I saw a _____

And a _____ danced in the park.

There was a _____ under the great green sky

And a _____ was scared of the dark.

The strange _____ roared loudly

And the _____ began to whine

The _____ jumped on the table

As the _____ sat down to dine.

Haiku

The haiku is a special sort of poem. It is just **one sentence** long and is split over **three lines**. It has a fixed number of **syllables** – **five** in the first line, **seven** in the second and **five** in the third. The idea is to give the reader a picture of one moment in time using just a few words. **For example:**

> Mountains in spring sun –
> Overlapping each other
> Yellow green all round.

Adapted from a haiku by **Masaoka Shiki** *(1869–1902)*

1. Here are two examples of haiku poems. Read the poems and picture the moment in time that they describe. Draw the picture in the boxes.

a) September sunshine –
The hovering dragonfly's
Shimmering shadow.

Adapted from a haiku by
Masaoka Shiki *(1869–1902)*

b) Silver, moonlit night –
the scent of melon flowers,
the sound of a fox.

Adapted from a haiku by
Kaya Shirao *(1738–1791)*

2. Here are the poems again. Mark the number of syllables in each line of the poem.

Sep/tem/ber sun/shine – [5]   Silver, moonlit night – [ ]

The hovering dragonfly's [ ]   the scent of melon flowers, [ ]

Shimmering shadow. [ ]   the sound of a fox. [ ]

Did you know... The haiku poem was invented hundreds of years ago in Japan. Matsuo Basho (1644–1694) was the first great haiku poet. The first haikus were about nature and the seasons. Now you can write a haiku about almost any subject, but the main idea remains the same.

Writing haiku poetry

The writer of a haiku must look closely at his or her surroundings and choose small but **interesting details** to write about. When you are writing a haiku you must **choose words carefully**. You will also need to experiment to make your words fit the **syllable pattern** of **5**, **7**, **5**.

I. Here is a haiku poem written without the line breaks:

In summer gardens, the distant lawnmower's drone lulls me into sleep

Write the haiku as it should be written – over three lines. The **syllable pattern** will help you.

_____

_____

_____

2. Arrange these words and phrases to make a **haiku** about the summer sun.

summer sun	people smile
winter gloom	softly
washes away	making

Summer sun haiku

_____

_____

_____

3. Write your own summer **haiku**. Choose a perfect summer moment to write about. Picture that moment and write your ideas in the box. Then write your ideas as a haiku.

Ideas for a summer haiku

Summer haiku

_____

_____

_____

In **shape poems**, the words are set out so that they **look like** the subject of the poem. A line of writing is twisted or words and phrases are set out so that they form the shape of the thing they are describing.

1. Here is an example of a shape poem for you to read.

Handy to Have

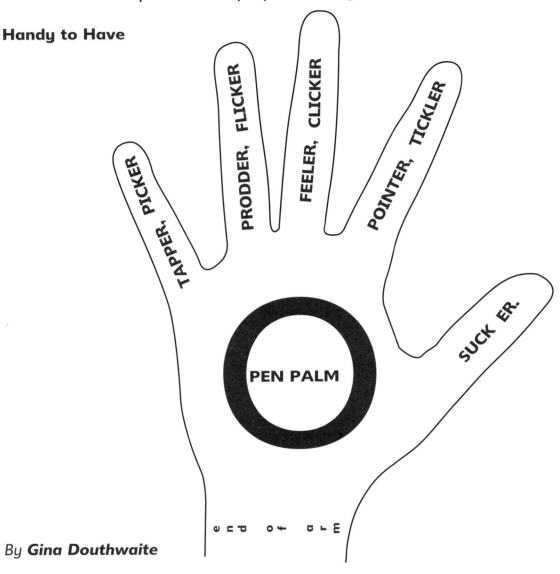

TAPPER, PICKER

PRODDER, FLICKER

FEELER, CLICKER

POINTER, TICKLER

SUCK ER.

PEN PALM

end of arm

By **Gina Douthwaite**

Look at how the poet has set out these parts of the poem. What do you notice?

'tapper, picker, prodder, flicker' _____

_____

'suck er' _____

'open palm' _____

Writing a shape poem

When you are writing a shape poem start by thinking of words and phrases to describe the subject. Then decide how these can be arranged to **make a picture** of the subject. You can use sentences twisted round to **follow the outline** of the shape. You can set out words and phrases to **look like the shape**. Or you can **fill the shape** with your words and phrases.

1. Write a shape poem about feet. Start by thinking of lots of words and phrases to describe feet:

Parts of feet:	Things feet do:	Words to describe feet:
sole	kick	kickers

2. Now trace this shape very lightly in pencil onto another piece of paper. Use the tracing to help you arrange your ideas into a shape poem. When you have finished your poem, carefully rub out the pencil line so that just the words remain.

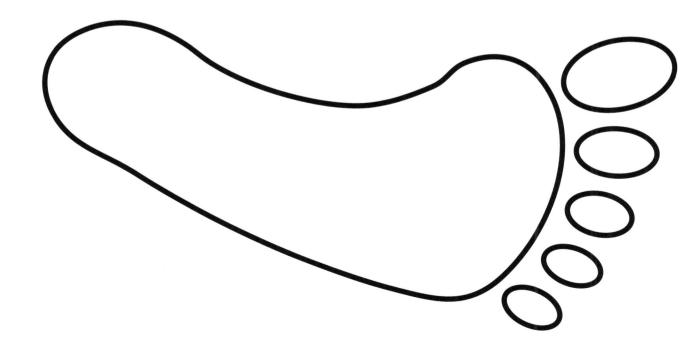

Narrative poems

A narrative poem **tells a story** and so it may be quite long. It describes a **series of events** about a character or an interesting happening. As in any story, a narrative poem can include dialogue. Because it is a poem, it will often use strong **rhythm** and **rhyme**.

1. Here is an example of a short narrative poem. It tells the story of a knight's lifelong search for a place called Eldorado – a place that was supposed to be full of gold. Unfortunately for the knight, Eldorado does not really exist.

Read the poem and think about what happens to the knight. Underline words and phrases that tell you about how the knight changes as his journey goes on.

Eldorado

Gaily **bedight**,
A gallant knight,
In sunshine and in shadow,
Had journeyed long,
Singing a song,
In search of Eldorado.

But he grew old –
This knight so bold –
And o'er his heart a shadow
Fell, as he found
No spot of ground
That looked like Eldorado.

And, as his strength
Failed him at length,
He met a pilgrim shadow:
'Shadow,' said he,
'Where can it be,
This land of Eldorado?'

'Over the mountains
Of the Moon,
Down the valley of the Shadow,
Ride, boldly ride,'
The shade replied,
'If you seek for Eldorado.'

By **Edgar Allen Poe** (1809–1849)

bedight – brightly dressed.

Responding to a narrative poem

1. What do you think the knight would have been thinking when he began his journey (verse 1)? Write your idea in the thought bubble.

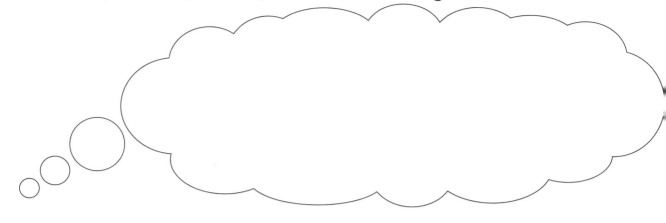

How would his thoughts have changed by the end of the poem?

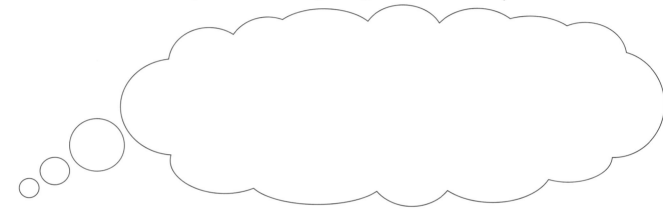

2. Look at these features of the poem. Write down what you notice.

The number of lines in each verse.	_____

The rhyme pattern in each verse.	_____

The last line of each verse.	_____

Did you know...? Some of the oldest poems are narrative poems. Thousands of years ago, people would tell stories about their history in poem form. One of the oldest known poems in the English language is called 'Beowulf'. It is written in Old English and is 3182 lines long. It tells the story of the hero, Beowulf, and his battles with monsters and dragons.

Poems in different forms

The **form** of a poem is its shape and how it is organised. There are many different forms of poetry and poems can come in all shapes and sizes. Some forms have fixed rhyme patterns, some have fixed syllable patterns and others have very few set rules.

1. Here are some poems about water. On the right you will find descriptions of different poem **forms**. See if you can match the poem with the correct description of its form.

a) What is it?

> Thirst quencher
> Fire extinguisher
> Plant reviver
> Bath filler
> Hand washer

An **acrostic** is a poem that spells out its subject by using the initial letters. The letters are often at the start of each line.

b) Water, Water

> **W**onderful water
> **A**lways there at the
> **T**urn of a tap
> **E**arth's gift to us –
> **R**ivers, lakes, seas and oceans
>
> **W**hy do we waste water?
> **A**lways using more
> **T**han we need.
> **E**mpty reservoirs and
> **R**iver beds dried up

A **kenning** describes or gives clues about a subject, but does not say what it is. The clues are often two words long, for example, a cat might be a *mouse chaser*.

c) Water

> Splashing,
> Rushing, spraying
> Thrown high into the air
> Diamond drops glinting in sunlight –
> Water.

A **limerick** is a five-line poem that is usually funny. The first, second and last lines all rhyme, while line 3 rhymes with line 4. Most limericks are about people. Some, but not all, begin: 'There was a young ... from ... '

d) Jane the Drain

> Mrs Wilson's naughty daughter
> Has used every drop of water –
> Not a dribble does remain.
> Unless, soon, it starts to rain
> We really will have to report her.

A **cinquain** is a five-line poem with a fixed number of syllables in each line (2 syllables in the first line, then 4, 6, 8, 2).

Writing poems in different forms

Sometimes you might think of a **subject** for your poem and then decide on a **form** that will suit it. Sometimes you might decide on the **form** and then think of a suitable **subject**. Try working in both ways and see which way works best for you. Use the ideas and poems in this book to start you off.

1. Decide on a **subject** for a poem. In the box, write down words, phrases and ideas that come into your head when you think about that subject.

Subject:

2. Now form your ideas into a poem. Write your poem in two different forms and decide which works best. For example, you might try an acrostic and a haiku, or a cinquain and a kenning.

Poem 1:

Poem 2:

Kennings are an ancient form of word play, often used in Old English and Old Norse poetry. Sometimes, kennings were used to describe people (e.g. *war-bringer*) as well as to describe objects (e.g. *oar-steed* to describe a ship; *God's beacon* to describe the sun).

Now you try!

Here are some ideas that you can try at home for reading and writing poetry.

Poetry collection

Start a collection of your **favourite poems**. Copy out the poem if it is short, or an extract from it if it is a longer poem. You can then decide how you think the poem should be illustrated. You could try making your collection of poems into a book.

Poetry reading

Organise a poetry reading where friends or members of your family can read or perform their favourite poems. You could even **learn a poem** off by heart to perform at the poetry reading. Choose a poem with a strong **rhythm** and **rhyme** – this makes it easier to remember.

Pop music lyrics

Remember there has always been a link between **songs** and **poetry**. Listen to or read the lyrics to some pop songs. See if you can find examples of **rhyme**, **rhythm**, **sound patterns** or **images** used in the lyrics. Then try writing your own pop song!

Rhymes

Rhymes turn up in all sorts of odd places. For example, have you ever noticed how many advertisements use **rhymes**? Sometimes we make up rhymes without realising it ('I'm a poet, and I didn't know it!') Start collecting interesting rhymes.

Collecting ideas

To write poetry you need lots of interesting ideas. Ideas for poems can come to you at any time so start a **poetry notebook** where you can jot down your ideas before you forget them. Take it with you, particularly if you are going on a journey where you might have lots of thinking time.

Rhymes for a reason

Try writing poems for special occasions – for example, a friend's birthday, or your baby brother's first tooth. Write the poem in a card so that the person you give it to can keep a copy of it. Of course, the poem does not have to rhyme – it could be a cinquain or an acrostic... or whatever form you choose